CHANGING THE
CHATTER

Help your daughter look beyond the mirror for better self-esteem.

Alicia Marcos Birong

E T C
PUBLISHING

Published by ETC Publishing

www.etcpublishing.com

ISBN 978-1-944622-04-6

Cover design by Lauren Motley

Concepts presented in this book are derived from the author's life experiences and education in the fields of counseling and life coaching. They are intended to be informative and to introduce a sound method of establishing a firm self-esteem foundation in young girls. Neither the author nor the publisher makes any claim that *Changing the Chatter* participants are inured against hardship, but we are certain that the program provides tools for approaching adulthood with confidence.

*I dedicate this book to
my family, past and present,
to the Sisters of St. Mary of Namur
and to the many friends, families and youth
who've supported me along my journey.*

Contents

Foreword

Congratulations. You have made an enlightened decision to acquire a book about the ChatterGirls experience. It makes me glad to write these few words to you about it.

About thirty years ago, three things began to come together in my professional and personal life that have helped me appreciate this text.

First, I was introduced, in some depth, to the theory and approach of cognitive psychotherapy. Simply put, this inner talk counseling model (which can also be utilized in some cases as a self-help technique) is a means of helping persons—of various ages—appropriate and adopt the power to think about and deal with the things of life, especially developmental complications and problems, in practical and constructive ways. Ultimately, it can be a powerful self-esteem building engine.

Second, I began in the mid-1980s to eagerly read the works of Erik Erikson, Lawrence Kohlberg, David Elkind, and Carol Gilligan—to name a few specialists who centered on the psycho-social and moral development of boys and girls. This long literary inquiry eventually led me to the insights of Sheila Green and, more recently (as the new grandfather of a little girl), to the 'girl talk' and 'tweenage makeover' concepts of Haley Kilpatrick and Michelle Icard.

The third factor was that I met Alicia Marcos Birong around 1983 while we each had helping profession jobs in the New Orleans area. It became obvious to me, very quickly, that she had a deep affection and emotional resonance for all youth—especially the early adolescent stage often labeled these days as 'tweens' (which is sometimes used as a derogatory term), pre-teens, and the youngest Millennials. It was also apparent that Alicia's growing concern for the travails of modern young people—coupled with her own experience of the tween, teen, and young adult years—might morph into a career/life commitment dedicated to understanding and helping kids. Over time, her deep interest in the healthy development of young females came particularly to the fore. It has been most interesting to watch these changing seasons of Alicia's vocation, over 30+ years, come to be and blossom naturally, like the dynamic seasons of a human being's developmental journey.

You will find all three of these themes integrated well into this book and into the overall ChatterGirls program. The careful attempt to educate and empower young women as to how to think about themselves and engage the world; the culled wisdom of thinkers and writers layered through the sections; and the practical insights of a writer and facilitator who carries decades of experience with a therapist's skill and a minister's heart—yes, they are all in here, as you will easily recognize.

So, you are probably holding a book about ChatterGirls mostly because you wish to help some young girl(s) cope with the social and inner pressures that go with growing up, and to appropriate some life skills that will lead them toward responsible young womanhood.

Make the most of that valorous mission. This resource will assist you.

Reynolds R. Ekstrom
Louisville, Kentucky

*~ Today, I look at my challenges, and
I remember that each positive step I take
carries me toward the life of my dreams. ~*

Introduction

When you look in the mirror, who looks back?

Is she smiling, confident, eager to face the day? Is she certain of her value, secure in the knowledge of her worth? Or does she frown, fixated on flaws, listening to an inner voice that says "Why bother," "You don't measure up," or even "You are one ugly failure?"

Does she consistently make mindful choices, walking a path that extends respect, compassion and love to others—as well as to herself?

Everyone falters, that's for sure. We all learn as we go. But some seem far more destined to repeat mistakes that seriously wound, and may even kill. The question is why?

I'm Alicia Marcos Birong, and I've made it my life's work to key in on this question, particularly as it relates to girls and young women. I've studied the answer, and I've developed the most effective response: prevention.

We need to prevent those common adolescent and pre-adolescent feelings of inadequacy from taking root, and replace them with budding self-assurance, self-reliance and self-confidence, as well as empathy for others. Through a five-step program I've developed called *Changing the Chatter: Celebrating ChatterGirls*, today's young girls can learn not only to be secure in their knowledge of self-worth, but also to be champions for their peers, consistently building one another up throughout the precarious path of the teen and pre-teen years.

My focus on youth began in the youth ministry of the Catholic Church back in my Texas hometown. I went on to become a certified youth minister, and today, my background includes a master's degree in counseling, life coaching and hypnotherapy certifications, pediatric hypnotherapy expertise, instructional experience and nationwide speaking exposure.

More importantly, though, I'm a fiercely strong woman who sees in the mirror a person of great value.

But that wasn't always the case. In fact, for decades, it was far from it. I spent my younger adult years mired in the very sort of muck I'm now determined to help young girls to avoid.

In my practice, I work with both children and adults. And I've discovered far too many women in their 30s, 40s and even 50s who've traveled a self-destructive road borne of the same foundation or, more accurately, the lack thereof.

Psychologists have found that a woman's self esteem takes root between the ages of 8 and 14. Plant the right seeds during that time span, and the benefits are both immediate and lifelong. Fail, and the fallout is equally enduring.

Sadly, for some, the defeating effects of low self-esteem lead to years of failed relationships, career crashes, addictions and worse. Studies show that a girl who emerges from adolescence with poor self-esteem likely will be at least 30 before she has a shot at changing it.

Imagine two young women in their late teens or early 20s, one who has high self-esteem and one who does not. Each will make a series of key life choices by the time she reaches her 30s—everything from choosing a career path to selecting a mate and possibly starting a family.

The empowered, confident woman is far less likely to fall into or remain in an abusive relationship or, for that matter, a relationship that is simply not right for her. She'll choose a career based on aptitude and pursue with self-assurance the education necessary to achieve it. She'll meet challenges head-on, knowing that she's mentally equipped to overcome.

She greets her 30s having built on her already solid self-esteem foundation, and having accomplished much. If she's chosen to be a mom, she's the one raising daughters with an equally strong sense of their own self-worth.

The other young woman heads into young adulthood at a severe disadvantage. She may pass on the most golden of opportunities, frozen by fear of failure, certain that trying leads only to disappointment. She is vulnerable to the slightest show of affection, figuring she's not deserving of great love, respect or admiration. She's the far more likely candidate for victimization, substance abuse and yes, even suicide.

Assuming she makes it, she approaches her 30s saddled with the baggage of a broken or failing marriage, or perhaps bearing the mental and physical scars of surviving a string of abusive relationships. Maybe she is raising children, attempting to provide love though she has not yet learned to truly love herself. Women in this category often also turn to alcohol or illegal drugs to numb the depression that accompanies a deepening sense of self-loathing.

Wouldn't it be better to prevent such a path from developing for our daughters? Let's equip them with the tools necessary to love the person they see in the mirror; remove their masks; change the negative chatter; find their voice; and be 100 percent themselves, secure in the knowledge that they are 100 percent great. And let's do it when it really matters, while they still are building the sense of self-worth that they will carry into adulthood.

This would be the greatest gift we could give our girls. Wouldn't it?

This is precisely why I developed *Changing the Chatter*, and why I want to see new ChatterGirls chapters bloom across the nation, perhaps the world. I want to help young girls everywhere to become empowered women—women who are as comfortable in a boardroom as in a classroom, who express themselves fearlessly, and who learn from and avoid repeating mistakes.

I know all too well the fallout they face if the self-worth framework is faulty. I spent nearly 40 years behind a mask, putting on an outward appearance of wellbeing, while internally, my soul cringed and my decision-making suffered.

In this book intended for adults interested in *Changing the Chatter* for their daughters, I offer a glimpse of my deeply personal reasons for developing this important life-skills system. It is my hope that readers will come away with a better understanding of my commitment to this cause, and a yearning to share the movement with other moms and dads, uncles, aunts or grandparents.

~ The chatter in my mind sometimes seems overwhelming,
but I have the power to change it. I need only to
remember what CHATTER stands for: ~
Celebrating
Happy
Aspiring
Truthful
Thoughtful
Esteem
Respect

Chapter 1

What We Do

Changing the Chatter: Celebrating ChatterGirls consists of five, two-hour-long, small-group sessions of up to 10 girls ages 8 to 10, or 11 to 14. A single instructor with a strong background in working with children guides the participants through exercises, such as role-play, contemplative time and creating crafts that reinforce lessons.

Each session focuses on the day's topic, including: *Mirror, Mirror (What Do You See?); Behind the Mask; Changing the Chatter; My Voice;* and *100 Percent ME.*

The program helps young girls to establish values and adopt skills to thwart negative internal and external, social pressures. The result is a young woman with a solid foundation on which to build a strong, confident future.

Other self-esteem-building programs exist, and each has its own merit. This program employs trained, older teen peer leaders, and aims to offer practical guidance and tools to build and affirm positive self-esteem. Among its components are many take-home tools, including a unique set of CDs or downloadable MP3s that participants can use to review *Changing the Chatter*'s key points again and again.

Who enrolls their daughters in *Changing the Chatter: Celebrating Chattergirls*? They may be parents who've noticed that their daughter is growing withdrawn or displaying signs of anxiety, deep sadness, anger or other self-destructive behavior.

Ultimately, though, the only requirement is that they're parents who are genuinely concerned about offering their girls the right toolbox for thriving throughout adolescence and beyond.

Changing the Chatter is for every girl, whether or not she's exhibiting signs of struggle.

Follow-up conversations with past participants and their mothers confirm that *Changing the Chatter: Celebrating ChatterGirls* works. Not only do the girls continually employ the skill set learned and tools developed during their ChatterGirls experience, they also frequently settle into a quiet spot and soak in the meditative, re-affirming messages provided on the CDs.

Thirteen-year-old Maddie and her sister, 11-year-old Anabelle, were among the first to participate in the program in 2013, when Maddie was 11 and Anabelle was 9. Their mother, Kelly, said she believes the need exists for all young girls to participate in *Changing the Chatter.*

It helped her daughters, she said, to develop a strong and confident inner voice that combats all sorts of negative pressures—allowing them to thwart go-along-to-get-along demeanors, defy unhealthy self-image messaging, and to speak up for themselves when others encourage them to do something they know is wrong.

Both of the girls said, two years later, that they frequently pulled out their CDs to reinforce the lessons learned.

"It's a little reminder to help you along the way," Maddie said. "Our friends who come over like to do this relaxation thing and we all listen to the CDs."

Each also still puts her ChatterGirls toolbox to excellent use.

"It helps me at school," Maddie said. "I'm in a play right now, and if it weren't for ChatterGirls, I wouldn't be able to handle it as well. I have that confidence booster. I'm not red in the face when I'm up there. I'm more my natural self."

Anabelle also is thankful for the lingering effects of her ChatterGirls experience.

"I think ChatterGirls helped me to speak up," she said. "Before, I didn't want to embarrass myself. Now I'm not afraid.

"ChatterGirls also helps me when I'm feeling low," she continued. "I think about what we did and try to help myself to think positive thoughts about myself."

Kelly said that as her daughters continue to mature, they pull out their ChatterGirls tools as needed to meet everyday challenges.

"It certainly helped the girls to identify certain feelings that contribute toward their outward behavior," she said. "Even now, let's say if they're feeling crabby for instance, they'll go to a quiet place in their room and listen to the CDs. They know there's something about those that helps them gather their thoughts, take a deep breath and go forward."

So, just what is a ChatterGirl?

Through the *Changing the Chatter* program, a Chatter-Girl becomes one who **C**elebrates life's shining moments, everything from birthdays to goal-setting, scoring well on a test or helping a friend over a hurdle. She is **H**appy, choosing to see the good, or at least the lesson, in every situation and sharing her positive and encouraging nature with others.

She **A**spires to do her best at any task, and develops a plan for achieving goals, inspiring others as an example of what can be achieved through effort. Even in her early and sometimes failed attempts at mastering a skill, her determination and forward steps can change her life or someone else's.

She is **T**ruthful, honest with herself and with others, removing her mask and proudly displaying who she is. It is the truthful girl who realizes that she is unique in every way, and who honors this by opening herself up to others and recognizing their inherent value. She's also Thoughtful, ready to help and support others.

The thoughtful girl has the chance to change the world. She learns about her own personal challenges, adapts and overcomes, and shows all who know her the power of her perseverance.

She exhibits a high self-Esteem; she knows she has great value and purpose. She is Responsible, considerate of the wishes of others, but always thinking, choosing and behaving based on what is most healthy and best for her.

How does she arrive here?

Changing the Chatter: Celebrating ChatterGirls offers a five-step process, with ample time during each program session for reflection; positive, esteem-building encouragement; safe sharing; a quiet, calming technique I call "Journey to the Mind" (supplemented with take-home CDs or downloadable MP3s); fun activities that are designed to reinforce lessons; journaling; and ChatterTime, when the girls are free to talk and discuss what they've learned or what's happening in their lives

*~ Removing my mask shows courage. It takes time.
I work at it daily, and as I do, I grow stronger. ~*

Chapter 2

Where it Started

Too many of us fixate on what we see as lacking when we check our reflection in the mirror. We see hair that's too curly or too straight, skin that's too blemished, a nose that's too big, ears that stick out, a body that's nothing like the fashion-model ideal ...

For a young girl, the mirror can be a dreadful minefield. The simple act of brushing hair or teeth may bring about the internal replay of a bully's taunt. Constant exposure to everything from movies to mobile devices reinforces the notion of not stacking up.

How can *Changing the Chatter* help? Who will it help?

One of the beauties of the program is that its lessons apply as equally to the bright, outgoing girl growing up in a loving home with two devoted parents as to the introvert whose grades are flagging and whose home life's in upheaval. It applies to the girl who likes her reflection in the mirror and to the one who loathes it.

In short, every young girl everywhere can benefit. For all girls, the chance to establish or reaffirm a positive self-esteem foundation, to be equipped with tools readying them for life's inevitable challenges, is an opportunity not to be missed.

When I think about the roots of *Changing the Chatter*, I reflect upon my own development. The chatter in my head growing up was predominantly negative.

The sounds of shouting, screaming, broken glass and smashed furniture are among my earliest memories. Dad routinely screamed at mom, furiously frustrated with her seeming inability to grasp his latest message. Both threw things at each other, including punches.

My younger brother and I spent many a night cowering and running for our beds. There, pulling the blankets over our heads, we'd cry ourselves to sleep, muffling the screaming and yelling, crashing and banging going on just beyond our doors. These frightening scenes so frequently repeated that eventually they sort of melted into the background, becoming little more than slightly disturbing white noise. I didn't understand back then, growing up in Fort Worth, Texas, in the '50s, that my outwardly stunning mom suffered inwardly from mental illness.

Dad, meanwhile, was ill-equipped to cope—either with her or with us. His response to my mother's storminess was to stay later and later at work.

It would be many years before I grasped why our household was so different from those of my peers around the neat, middle-class neighborhood. While their moms cleaned house and cooked meals—and even cuddled and played with them—mine drank coffee, smoked cigarettes and brooded.

She was ill, I'd come to learn, trapped in a place of anger and despair or lost in a cloud of nicotine and fantasy. Either way, she just wasn't present, wasn't emotionally there. By the time I was 6, the household chores, including caring for my then-infant brother, had fallen to me.

I had no time after school for homework, nor a nice, quiet space for studying. That, combined with undiagnosed dyslexia, led to poor grades, further eroding my already flagging self-esteem.

To this day, I do not believe that other adults don't know or suspect what goes on behind closed doors in families like mine. I always felt that my teachers knew something was wrong. They weren't sure how to help, though they tried. Some would see me sitting alone at recess, and they'd stop to sit and talk with me.

I really was not aware of the dysfunction in my own home until I visited other girls' houses. They always said "Oh, your mom is so beautiful; you're so lucky." And then, I'd shrink and withdraw. My mother's beauty was overwhelming to me, further convincing me that I was just an ugly, injured duckling trying to stay afloat in her world.

Everyone faces some sort of childhood struggle. Some have it better, and many have it worse. My brother and I, for example, didn't starve for food. We weren't locked in closets or whipped or molested. But children need emotional nourishment, too, and when it's lacking, the effects are damaging and long-term.

I remember looking in the mirror as a child, and being so unhappy at the reflection of an awkward girl with big, ugly glasses. Mom had no sense of my struggles; dad had no skills to help me see what was beautiful. He said years later that he just didn't know how to handle a daughter. He'd hoped to count on mother for that.

She did not—could not—rise to the occasion.

Tagging along on things like fishing outings with dad might have boosted my sense of belonging and wellbeing. But, because I was a girl, these invitations did not come.

He did, however, teach me to ride a bike. I was 12, older than most to achieve that milestone, but it is among my fondest childhood memories.

I also remember enjoying summertime get-togethers with my brother and our cousins in Wichita Falls, Texas, where, oddly enough, grown-ups didn't scream or throw things at each other, and they generally treated us kids as though we were special.

We spent hot, sunny days on my grandmother's farm, where her drape-making business was spread across a cutting board in the middle of the living room. My cousins and I sometimes would hang out under there, our little fort beneath the folds of fabric.

Childhood bumped along this way, primarily with my parents feuding and my brother and I fending for ourselves, until it all came to an awful head shortly after I graduated from high school.

I was 18 and my brother was 12 when my father left our mother and moved to an apartment in town.

Not long after that, my mother attempted suicide.

I was 6 when it fell to me to care for my younger brother. At 18, I had to sign the commitment papers that sent my mother to a psychiatric care facility.

It was a traumatizing childhood. But it also was the beginning of my journey, part of what's shaped me. For many years, it shaped me for the worse. But this and the other experiences of my youth also provided me with a profoundly deep understanding of what it means to enter adulthood without a solid self-esteem basis. It is what has compelled me to build a life of helping others and, in particular, young girls.

When I think about *Changing the Chatter*, I think about how nobody outside of our home truly knew what I faced as I was growing up. No one understood what was happening behind the scenes as I struggled to keep up at school. No one knew my story, so how could they effectively care or comfort or encourage?

Raised Catholic, I attended parochial school, and I threw myself into church activities. My earliest glimmers of possessing any sense of self-worth I trace to my interactions with some of the nuns, and, in my late teens, to gaining a ministry position working on the Happening Team through my local parish. I became a counselor for youths making their way through their own self-searching.

It was in helping others, in realizing that sense of reward and receiving positive feedback, that I first glimpsed my calling. But it would be decades before I'd truly achieve it.

That crucial 8- to 14-year-old period had come and gone for me without the setting of a strong self-esteem foundation. In fact, quite the opposite was true. And I'd learned early on to put on the mask and behave as if everything was just fine.

~ Everyone makes mistakes.
Life is about learning from them. ~

Chapter 3

Walk Toward Wisdom

Women who arrive at adulthood's door with low self-esteem face a rocky road. I know, because I traveled it.

Nowadays, I am proud of how it's all turned out. I have a wonderful husband, two great, well-adjusted adult children whom I adore, and two grandchildren who also fill my heart.

I have my successful counseling, hypnosis and life-coaching practice. And, thanks to the understanding and empathy I developed along my journey, I now also have *Changing the Chatter: Celebrating ChatterGirls*.

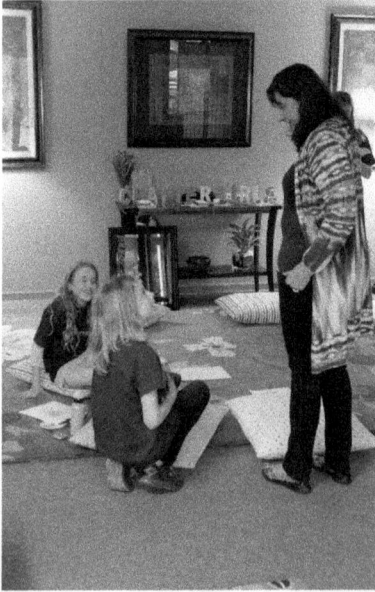

A life spent helping others is a richly rewarding one. I am lucky.

But to say I always made the best choices and have no regrets would be untrue. I was 22 years old when I married my first husband—so young, and yet, at the time I considered myself an old maid. We both were introverts back then, so it seemed to fit. But the marriage would end after a little more than a decade.

In fact, between the ages of 22 and my early 40s, I endured a string of failed relationships with men—one of which involved an inordinately manipulative and abusive man with whom I stayed for far too long.

As I look back on it all, the emotion that ruled me was fear. I feared failure. I feared I would not be a good mom. I feared I would fail as a wife. I also feared the growing sense within that I'd brought children into the world before I'd really figured out who I was or who I wanted to be.

One thing I did learn early on was that my ability to listen to others—truly listen—was a gift. I love being with young people. So I became a youth minister. I was so happy to serve God and to be a mom that, for a time, I believed I had the best of all worlds. But, while I was trying to balance these two roles, I was struggling as a wife. My three-legged chair had one termite-riddled limb.

My own upbringing did not exactly set the healthy-relationship example for marriage. In terms of being a spouse, I often felt so miserable inside that I wanted to die. While things were looking up for me in terms of career—I so loved my work with the junior high ministry—things at home simply grew worse and worse. Our marriage had been one between fellow introverts. Through my role at the church, I'd begun to be far more social. I needed to be able to be a public speaker. I received positive feedback, began to love it, and was growing as a person enjoying both external- and self-regard.

For work, I had to interact with all of the kids and their parents—with everyone. I had to come out of my shell, and I did. In my house, however, my budding self-esteem became just another source of conflict.

I looked around at the families in the pews at my church, and realized that my situation wasn't what it should be. I served the church, and sought direction within it. But in this, too, I failed. I was still that little girl inside, still searching for clues to the skills I hadn't been taught: how to be a mom, how to raise a family, how to be a wife, how to serve God.

Underlying it all was my lack of inner peace. My growing sense of self-acceptance and self-esteem in my work-a-day world was in constant conflict with my realization that my marriage was spiraling downward.

Outwardly, I served others cheerfully and well. Inwardly, the demons of my childhood dragged me to dark places.

Meanwhile, my husband began to travel more and more for work. When he was transferred to New Orleans, I hated the idea of leaving Arlington, Texas. But we went, at first with the agreement that I wouldn't work outside of the home. We'd work on the marriage, he said. For my own fulfillment, I found another church position, and even started a program there to become a certified youth minister.

I made some great friends in New Orleans, and began to build a sense of self. However, the more outgoing I became, the less my marriage worked. While my nature was shifting from introvert to sociable, my husband remained as he was, and we grew further and further apart. I decided that I had to leave our home.

"I don't know where I'm going, but I'm going," I told him.

Encouraged by friends to apply for a Diocesan position, I landed a job in Kalamazoo, Michigan, packed up the kids, and headed north. The job was a great opportunity. It wasn't the one I'd most wanted, but it was a terrific start toward a new life. There was just one problem. I knew then that I might want a divorce; the Diocese, however, required that I be married.

I talked with my husband about a separation. The kids were 7 and 9. Although I still was married on paper, for all intents and purposes, I became, at that point, a single mom.

I struggled through health issues, and received very little in the way of child support. Meanwhile, the Bishop kept asking when my husband would arrive in Kalamazoo. And in the end, he did come. We bought a house together, but the marriage was beyond resurrection.

Through all of it, my self-esteem ebbed and flowed, rising with my successes at the diocese and falling as I returned each night to an unloving household.

Realizing I needed to support my children, I started a pastoral counseling program, which I worked on during summers while my kids were in Texas with family. I later changed it to general counseling and continued to work on it for years while living in Georgia.

My time in Michigan was a time of great career growth, but also one of great pain as I grappled with the inevitability of my divorce, its effects on my children and its clash with my faith.

From Michigan, I moved on to another Diocesan position in Atlanta, where, again, I would experience the great highs of rewarding work, and the extreme lows of failed relationships.

If only I knew back when I left Texas as a struggling, soon-to-be single mom that I'd go on to live in eight states, meet hundreds of interesting people and work in so many counseling capacities. I suppose it was all part of God's plan to teach me survival and self-acceptance.

At the time, my awareness centered on just how tough single parenting can be. My less-than-great money management skills didn't help. I lost my identity and my faith so many times along the way. But I also learned from a variety of people that what's on the surface is not what we are all about.

Only when we dig deep and put in the effort not only to be our true selves, but also to love our true selves, can we be the person our children one day will admire and appreciate.

I failed in 50 percent of that, and succeeded in the other half.

I loved my kids, my church, my God. It was what kept me alive. But it seemed, for a long time, anyway, that any career-path gains were met with equal defeats in my personal life. As my career lurched forward, my relationships with men faltered. And, as hard as I tried to be a good mom, only my daughter maintains a close bond.

In the midst of my own trials, I learned to listen to others and to feel their pain while experiencing my own. I learned that I lived to serve others, but it came at a price, including low wages and long hours.

I worked in churches. I worked in retail. I worked with the poor and with the rich.

I learned that, in reality, very few of us have been taught the seemingly simple skill of liking ourselves, or that it's a choice we make. Regardless of any external influence that might lead us to believe otherwise, we must choose not just to like, but also to love ourselves.

This lesson took me years of trial by fire to learn.

~ There is absolute strength within the positive chatter in my mind, and it reminds me that I am in 100 percent control of me. ~

Chapter 4

Fight Fear

In Atlanta, I became director of the youth ministry for the Archdiocese.

I kept plugging away at the master's degree program through Loyola, and I took on part-time jobs to try to make ends meet for me and my children, both of whom were struggling with the fallout of their parents' failed marriage.

I worked for the Diocese Monday through Friday, had a part-time parish job as a youth minister, and took a part-time Neiman Marcus position selling Louis Vuitton handbags. By now, it was the late 1980s, and I also started my own party planning business called "Today's Events, Tomorrow's Memories".

During the course of my eight years in Atlanta, I finished my master's degree program, quit the church and retail jobs and kept my events business. I reconciled with my father, yet became involved with a man who was cruel and abusive. I tried to end that relationship multiple times, but kept returning.

In the midst of this, my then 16-year-old son left to go live with his father, and what little remained of my self-esteem at that point left with him.

I knew I needed to get away from the abusive man in my life. I had to make better personal-life choices, so I took my daughter and we moved outside of Atlanta to Peachtree City. There, I took another church job.

I struggled with depression, and I struggled at my job. I wasn't the strong, dependable, responsible worker I'd always been. I was 41, and about to become the unemployed single mom of an angry teen-age daughter and a slightly older son who'd chosen his father's house over mine.

I was devastated, but I knew I had to pull it together.

I found a job as a program director at a Christian-based substance-abuse treatment center. Once again, I was blessed with a good job. The pendulum on my professional life swung upward; the reverse remained true in my personal life. This had to change.

I so firmly believe that with a better self-esteem foundation, built at the right time during pre-adolescence, I'd never have become enmeshed in unhealthy relationships. I'd have made so many different and better choices, all along the way. But I also believe that this journey has been mine for a reason, and I thank God for the resolution of it all.

In this life, the love we receive or don't receive from others contributes or detracts. But if we believe in our minds that we are "less than" others, we'll never overcome life's challenges.

Without belief in self, we live in fear. Fear becomes anger.

We choose paths hoping to find happiness and fulfillment, but searching to claim either of these things from others without first finding them within ourselves is like trapping ourselves in a room with a false floor. We never know when it will give way, sending us tumbling into the black abyss.

When we change the chatter, we replace fear with confidence. We grow in the knowledge that our keys to happiness and fulfillment are not in others' hands. The keys are ours. They're in our hearts and minds. We can share our happiness with others. But we must never, ever hand over our keys.

In Atlanta, my keys seemed lost. But I began my search for them, knowing that once reclaimed, I'd be responsible for them from that moment on.

~ Change is sometimes difficult,
but it gives me the opportunity to grow. ~

Chapter 5

Renew, Heal, Grow

Determined to move on, I threw myself into my work. I became licensed in Georgia and started a private counseling practice. Importantly, I also began to see a counselor myself. For me, this was the beginning of true renewal, the start of a peeling away of the thick mask that I'd put on to cope. It wasn't going to be easy. It wasn't going to be quick. It was, however, going to be worth every minute.

The Olympics were coming to Atlanta that year. My daughter, then in college, joined me for a gathering in a Decatur, Georgia, park, not far from where I was living. It was opening night for the Olympics. A large screen was set up in the park and residents were invited to come and watch the opening ceremonies.

A man in front of me caught my eye as he played cheerfully with a child in the grass. He introduced himself as David. A massage therapist, he was in town to work with the equestrian team.

My daughter said, "Mom, you're flirting with him." Maybe I was. He just seemed so normal and unassuming and nice. I offered to show him around Atlanta while he was in town. For the next month, we saw a lot of each other. Because of his Olympic credentials, I enjoyed seeing some behind-the-scenes venues that were off-limits to most.

When it was time for him to return to his home in St. Petersburg, Florida, David said I had a place to stay should I ever wish to visit.

We kept in touch.

The day arrived not long after that when I decided that I needed to put Atlanta behind me. Florida beckoned. With David, I had a safe place to stay, and being near the waters of Tampa Bay and the Gulf of Mexico brought me a tremendous sense of peace. I walked the beach each day, thinking about where I'd been and, more importantly, where I was going.

Mostly though, I just breathed.

I decided that I didn't want to counsel anyone again until I'd wrestled my own demons. I took one job as a barista at a coffee house and another at a catering business. I focused all of my counseling thoughts inward. I worked on me. It was the first time in my life when I'd allowed myself this luxury, this time to search inward.

David and I liked each other, and we were friends, but that was it at that point. I think I finally recognized that I'd been foolish to start romantic relationships while I had so much unresolved stuff stirring within.

While David pursued acupuncture school, I became extremely close friends with the catering business's administrative assistant, Gracie. After I'd been there just a couple of months, I learned Gracie was dying of breast cancer. I took Gracie every day to treatment and continued to work at the catering company. I was happy there.

Gracie taught me so many lessons about life. She also helped me to bring God back into my life as she prepared to die. I'd been dying, too, in my own way. But through her courage, I learned to live again.

After about a year, David and I began a romantic relationship. Meanwhile, he'd discovered that the acupuncture
program in Florida wasn't accredited, and he wanted
certification. He looked into programs in San Diego, California, and Santa Fe, New Mexico. Soon we were off to
Santa Fe, incorrectly believing it to be the less expensive of
our choices.

I didn't know it at the time, but Santa Fe would prove to
be a place of tremendous healing for me, a place where I'd
relinquish past hurts and build on a career of service in a
truly remarkable way.

~ I am not the girl who is afraid of the world.
I am the girl who gives of herself
to make life better for others. ~

Chapter 6

Look Forward

Santa Fe was beyond beautiful. Most people we came to know there were artists of one sort or another, and most worked two to three jobs to make ends meet.

It was an experience, to be sure. A close friend and confidante has said to me, "Alicia, in Santa Fe, you became you. You purged. You let go."

She's right. It was in Santa Fe that I reconnected with my mother, with whom I hadn't spoken since I lived in Atlanta. My mother long had retained an unhealthy grip on my psyche. But the verbal acid she spewed during a particular visit in Atlanta—where she shouted to me, my children and several of my employers that I was an awful person and a terrible mother—slammed our communication door shut for years.

This time, our conversations were different. I chose to communicate with my mother as part of my healing process, on my terms.

Santa Fe is also where I started hypnosis school, something I'd long wanted to do. Part of our training was to practice on one another. The subconscious mind is fascinating. It was an intensive, months-long program. And by the end of it, I'd released so much from my own complicated past while gaining a passion for what I saw as an excellent therapeutic method.

Known as a place of beauty and healing, Santa Fe was ideal for starting a hypnosis practice. I opened offices in Santa Fe and Albuquerque, and also worked in a catering business.

My hypnosis instructor knew I had a strong background in working with youth through my former church positions, and began to refer parents with struggling children my way. The youngest was 7.

I worked with adults and children. Many of David's fellow acupuncture students sought me out for help with memory retention and test anxiety. Among the children, attention-deficit disorder and attention-deficit-hyperactivity disorder was a frequent concern. Parents were interested in ways of helping their children without turning to pharmaceuticals. So was I. Word got out that my techniques were uniquely helpful; some parents drove great distances from neighboring states to seek me out.

Hypnosis had grown popular by then as a method to assist with weight loss and smoking-cessation. But my leanings veered less and less in those directions and more and more in the direction of assisting children grappling with everything from ADD to crippling anxiety, post-traumatic-stress disorder and eating disorders. I developed scripts for both children and adults to empower them to change their lives significantly for the better.

The cases I worked on were fascinating. And my success in the youth ADD/ADHD arena garnered notice from area school systems, which hired me to teach their teachers methods of helping struggling students.

David and I spent four years in Santa Fe, from 1996 to 2000. For me, it was a tremendous time of helping others to heal and grow while doing a great deal of my own healing and growing, too. As the decade ended, though,

David decided he was going to return to Florida, while I yearned to head further west. We parted ways as friends. I'll always appreciate our time together as one of great personal growth and the realization that relationships need not be unhealthily one-sided.

When I left Santa Fe for California, I was unsure of precisely where I'd land. But I finally was secure in who I was and who I wanted to be. I'd left behind all of my crud from my childhood, all of my pain and guilt from past relationship failures. My mask was gone. And I was ready, for the first time in my adult life, to thoroughly believe in myself.

I was in my 40s, and my life was just beginning.

It shouldn't have to take that long. It doesn't have to take that long.

~ Aspiring begins in my heart,
happens in my mind,
and is realized in my words and deeds. ~

Chapter 7

Cultivate Connections

After visiting for about a month with some relatives who lived in San Jose, California, I settled in San Diego. From connections I'd made in a spiritualists' church in Santa Fe, I knew that a like-minded group met in San Diego, and among the first things I did was to introduce myself to them.

They were wonderful people, and helped me to find a place to stay.

I also completed pediatric hypnosis specialty training during weekends in Santa Clara.

It was late spring of 2000. I was 48, and I was ready to forge both professional and personal commitments.

I met a friend who was a chiropractor and who'd been in hypnosis school with me in Santa Fe. He worked with a life coach who was opening his own office and had space to share. It was in that space that I began my practice. I became intrigued with life coaching and how that might meld with hypnosis, so I pursued and achieved life coach certification as well.

Things really began to take off, as word spread of the life-changing work I was doing with children who needed to break away from debilitating patterns, such as cutting, refusing healthy foods and more.

I saw clients, and also began teaching pediatric hypnosis.

Importantly, I noticed as I worked with young people that the common thread with all of them was low self-esteem.

Whatever the outward expression of their suffering might be, it always came down to providing them with the tools necessary to establish and maintain self-confidence.

The results I achieved gained notice, and soon I received calls from the San Diego schools. I developed a six-week program for ADD and ADHD. In six sessions, I could turn a kid around. Occasionally I worked with children beyond six weeks, but within that time period, I was able to steer them clear of medical interventions.

The combination of life-coach training, extensive youth counseling experience and my pediatric hypnosis background proved to be highly effective in working with children who'd suffered traumas, been bullied and more.

I began to receive calls from all over California. Some parents even flew their children to San Diego for visits. I was invited to speak about pediatric hypnosis at American Council of Hypnotist Examiners' conferences.

For me, it was all a great new adventure. And I so loved the area, with its amazing bay views and balmy breezes.

Still, something was missing. I was ready, I knew, to share my life. I dated a bit, and wrote down the attributes of the sort of man my heart desired. Luckily for me, my roommate introduced me to just such a man, who's now my husband, Bill.

Like any couple, Bill and I faced struggles, the keenest of which came when he let me know that he needed to move back to northeastern Illinois, where his parents lived. I wasn't crazy about leaving San Diego, but I loved Bill very much. And I knew that my calling—my work with children—was something I could continually develop in any location.

So, we made the leap, marrying and moving to Crystal Lake, Illinois, in 2005. Bill is a licensed clinical social worker with a local hospital and a therapist at the practice we co-founded in Crystal Lake, Guided Choices.

For three years after our move, I returned once a month to see clients in San Diego. Even now, I still receive occasional emails from people I saw there who tell me that they regained control of their lives with my help.

It is through those experiences, through my own journey, and through the life-altering sessions that have followed at Guided Choices that I developed *Changing the Chatter.*

I know that this program works. I know that it instills in young girls the ability to take powerful control of their inner beings today and to continue to grow in self-esteem and confidence as they move forward.

I am 100 percent committed to ensuring that as many young girls as possible receive this program's tools and the know-how to use them.

~ As I think about the image that I see in the mirror, I will remember that it does not reflect the person within. I have the power to change, as well as to accept and embrace myself for who I am. ~

Chapter 8

Hide? No, Seek!

The reality is that no matter what kind of family one has—and there are no perfect families—most girls still, at some point in their lives, hide who they are. They mask their self-doubts, doubts that may creep into their minds not necessarily from big traumas, but from something as random as a classmate's demeaning comment about their dress that day.

Then they look in the mirror, and they see nothing but bad.

I have one young girl I've worked with who has the most beautiful hair. Yet, she'd sit before the mirror and say, "I hate my hair. I'm ugly."

If the inner beauty is not developed, then the outer beauty never happens for these girls. It's stifled, and that's when they allow the chatter to control them, and they don't find their voices. I don't think I found my voice, my real voice, until after I was 40 years old.

I used hypnosis after years of counseling, and it was the only thing that allowed me to let go of my childhood traumas. Until I did that, they just kept damaging me—with relationships, with men, with my children, with many situations in my life.

The reality is, the way society is now, even girls from the healthiest of homes start having a variety of difficult experiences at a young age. There's the age-old pressure to fit in and the pain associated with not being counted among the "it crowd." Add to that cyber bullying and the constant media spotlight on who looks great and who doesn't.

Too many women who walk through my door today still are dealing with decades-old traumas. They've allowed these traumas to rule them. I understand, because I've been where they are, but I also know that this long-term suffering, and the poor decision-making that goes with it, are preventable.

Changing the Chatter helps participating ChatterGirls to learn to deal with such issues and experiences now, so that they can head toward adulthood feeling healthy and strong.

"I think young girls struggle because it's at a point where little cliques start to form, some people start to think they're superior, bullying starts to come out," said Maddie, who, at 13, said she looked forward to high school, in large part due to her ChatterGirls experience.

"With ChatterGirls you can start to see that you don't need to use (popular girls or celebrities) as role models," she said. "I'll be who I want to be."

Her mother said she is impressed with the way both of her daughters handle themselves and continually employ their ChatterGirls tool sets to reveal their true selves and develop positive relationships with classmates.

Is your daughter exhibiting the symptoms of hiding behind a mask? Is she growing withdrawn or exhibiting anger? Does she avoid rather than tackle challenging schoolwork? Has she said things like "My teacher doesn't understand me," or "I can't learn this math from that dumb teacher; he never makes sense." In short, has she blamed others for her shortcomings?

Such actions are among classic coping mechanisms for someone suffering from low self-esteem. A mask of resentment may feel better than fear of inability. A mask of indifference might shield a girl from the gnawing wounds of bullying. A mask of toughness might cover anything from abuse to mishandled grief.

My program helps young girls to recognize that they or their classmates might reach for masks thinking them to be a quick fix. But what they really need is to learn how to tackle underlying issues. It's only by removing masks that we can truly grow and improve.

~ What happens when I look at a mirror?
Do I like what I see, and smile?
Or do I frown? ~

Chapter 9

Mirror, Mirror

As previously mentioned, "Mirror, Mirror" is the theme of the first session of *Changing the Chatter: Celebrating ChatterGirls.*

Part of the first session always is devoted to getting to know one another and allowing the girls (ages 8 to 10 or 11 to 14) to gain a comfort level with the program. A warm, inviting, casual atmosphere greets participants—with big pillows on the floor, one for each girl. A female high school student helps out with the various activities, with a ratio of at least one high school student per 10 girls.

At the first meeting, each participant also receives a pouch with her name on it, as well as a journal, pens and pencils, a sparkly mirror and more.

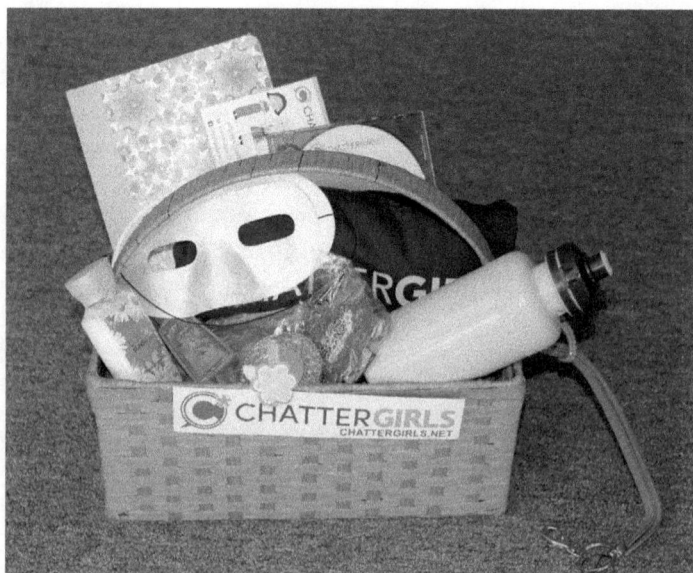

We talk about the program rules and responsibilities, centering on respecting one another, and the girls begin to learn how to introduce themselves and work on their individuality. Each girl tells a little bit about her family and herself. For example, "I'm Sarah and I have three brothers. My favorite color is purple. One of the things I like about myself is that I play hockey."

At that point, each girl takes out a piece of paper. The group leader has a big mirror and each girl spends one minute in front of it, sitting quietly, gazing into the glass. Each is asked to start journaling about who they see.

They're also asked to draw themselves, to depict themselves as how they believe they appear to others.

Just to look into the mirror is emotional for some girls. A minute is a long time. Many of the younger girls become nervous and might start laughing or giggling. It's a normal nervous response, and they generally overcome it rather quickly.

While one participant is in front of the large mirror, the rest are writing answers to the questions "What do you like most about yourself?" and "Who is the person you see in the mirror?"

After each one finishes her time in front of the mirror, she returns to her journal to finish the statements.

The girls have an opportunity to talk about and reflect upon who they are on the inside, who they see when they look in the mirror, and what they think others see. Is what others see different from how we view ourselves?

With groups of the older girls, we also talk about body image. Many times girls at this age are uncertain about what's happening with their bodies. We try to open that door so we can continue that discussion with the older girls throughout the program.

On the opposite side of their drawings of what they see when they look in the mirror, each girl draws herself as she believes others see her. These images can be stark. One girl in one of my earliest sessions drew a circle-slash symbol on the side describing how others see her.

Imagine how she must have been feeling—how truly in need she was of the ChatterGirls' set of self-image-correcting tools.

The girls are asked to look at their drawings of how they believe others see them, and to talk about whether they like that image. Does it make them sad? Does it make them smile? The girls then team up with partners to talk about it.

The ChatterGirls ask each other, "If you could change what you think others see, what would you change?" And we talk about this a bit more. If the girls could change the image of what they think others see, in what ways might they behave differently? For example, if others looked and saw a leader, would they be more driven to lead?

As a parent, you know that image is key throughout adulthood, as well. For young girls, the importance of self-image changes fairly drastically between the ages of 8 and 14. The 8- or 10-year-old might not care what she wears to school or whether her hair is combed.

We start to care early on, however, about how others treat us, and whether others are attracting the sort of attention we ourselves crave. While parental influence certainly factors strongly in the self-image of a young girl, peer behavior toward her takes on greater and greater prominence.

Many modern-day parents have grown less involved than their predecessors in their children's choices of friends. And we may feel powerless when we begin to notice the negative effects on our daughters when they face rejection or bullying. A girl might, for example, admire her classmate "Ann." She may perceive that Ann has the look, attitude and popularity that she'd like to cultivate.

So she may begin to dress like Ann and wear her hair like Ann, etc.

But if Ann sneers and scoffs at her, that rejection plays over and over in her mind. And suddenly another girl who was her friend when she was 5 also is rejecting her, because she, too, craves Ann's acceptance.

Perhaps you remember your own "Ann" from your middle school years. Ever wonder where she is today? Think about her. What has her journey been like? It's entirely possible this girl you most admired was wearing her own mask of sorts. Her cool, seemingly composed exterior might have hidden unknown emotional torments. If you sat with her now, she might surprise you with tales of her own inner critic.

Our harshest judgment always comes from within. We all have an inner critic. But that critic is fueled externally. How do you deal with your inner critic? Do you say negative things about yourself in front of your daughter?

When they first arrive at *Changing the Chatter*, many of the participants might not like the person they believe that others see.

Girls with lower self-esteem will tend to be very quiet. But through a variety of activities, and a portion of each session that I call "Journey to the Mind", we build each girl up and reinforce for her what an amazing and uniquely gifted person she is. Each ChatterGirl learns that she possesses attributes, strengths and abilities that are key to changing this world for the better. The trick, of course, is to develop them—boldly, fearlessly and with confidence.

At the end of each session we have "ChatterTime". Each girl shares one positive thing about each of the other girls in the room. So each girl departs at the end of the session having heard at least 10 positive things about themselves.

Actually, this positive sharing starts right up front. After the girls draw themselves, each of the other girls shares something they like about each picture.

From the very first experience, ChatterGirls are letting go of the negative, and working on building an inner bank of positive feedback—positive mind chatter. At the end of each session, the girls also receive CDs with reinforcing talk from the "Journey to the Mind" portion of the evening. It's something they can listen to on their own as needed. Many past participants have stopped me at the grocery store to tell me they continue to listen to their five CDs—one for each day of the school week—for months or even years afterward.

In keeping with the theme of the opening night, each girl is reminded that when she reaches for her new pocket mirror, what she'll see is beautiful inside and out.

Moms of ChatterGirls say that their daughters' attitudes change almost immediately, that the girls are so excited after the first night that they can't wait to come back. It's often a tremendous relief, as parents can feel so powerless in situations where their children are suffering. And, in fact, when it comes to changing the chatter and choosing a healthier self-image, a girl has to learn to do this for herself.

Helping girls to equip themselves to do just that is what *Changing the Chatter: Celebrating ChatterGirls* is all about.

"They were super enthused," said Kelly, mother of Maddie and Anabelle, as she reflected on her daughters' Chatter-Girls experience. "They always walked out of sessions very happy and wanting to tell me all about it."

It's an extremely gratifying response, though not surprising. Decades of both professional and personal enrichment have convinced this author that empowering young girls to believe in themselves will change the world.

~ The more I reveal of my true self to the world, the more self-assured I become. ~

Chapter 10

Remove the Mask

Few know as well as I the perils of dwelling behind the mask. I lost decades in this purgatory, and I'm devoted to sparing young women this fate.

As a coping mechanism or self-preservation tactic, many of us put up walls and false fronts. What we fail to recognize, however, is that to live behind a mask is to deprive ourselves of our own spiritual spark. I'm well aware of why it happens and how it happens. I'm equally aware that it's best avoided.

The mask for your daughter is much more than a mask. It's a barrier or shield, something she uses to comfort herself when anxiety peaks and self-esteem valleys. The more she puts on this front, the more it becomes the way others see and perceive her to be.

As a parent, you may begin to witness the disappearance of your little girl; a different one comes into view in social situations. The pressure to "fit in" is powerful. During program sessions, I see girls arrive with their masks and, happily, I witness them ending their sessions without it. They learn that they no longer need it. It serves no positive purpose.

Learning the true joy of living mask-free is a mental destination the girls must arrive at themselves. No one else can remove their masks for them, no matter how much you might wish it were possible.

A ChatterGirl learns to remove her mask on her own. She might reach for it occasionally under duress, particularly during her middle-school years. But it won't remain in place for long, because she knows she has the power within.

Let's build a world where young women don't feel the need to mask who they are to "get along." Let's make this a world where a girl with a knack for math or science won't downplay her talents to win a boy, where a girl has the skills to shrug off naysayers rather than shelving her dream of making it big in business or science or academia—or whatever she chooses.

What would the future be like if the young girls of today never felt the need to hide who they are, to bury insecurities or present themselves as pillars when inside, they're quaking? What would the future be like if far more of the young girls of today walked into the boardrooms of tomorrow brimming with self-assurance?

We may never prevent all young women from making self-defeating choices, but we can give them a far more dynamic launch into their young adult lives.

My own "springboard" into adulthood was more board than spring. I put the mask on early; make-believe felt better than truth.

Every day in my small Catholic school in Texas, the mask went on. No one needed to know what really was going on in my life outside of school. I didn't want to live that life, so I hid it. Except with God, sharing was not an option.

I hated going home after school, so I did whatever I could to stay late. When I did ride the bus home, I remember

sitting toward the back with some black friends. It was the
'50s, and this was the South. So, sure enough, I received
stares for my choice of companionship. Rather than stare
confidently back, secure in my spirit and in my place, I
buckled, behaving as if I didn't really know them.

The mask, once on, is difficult to rip away. Its damaging
effects can be long-term.

Unless we teach young girls to dispense with their masks,
to love themselves for who they truly are, this unhealthy
coping mechanism can manifest itself in all manner of
ways: anxiety, poor grades, stealing, behavioral problems,
obsessive-compulsive disorder, eating disorders, depression, suicidal thoughts, cutting and more.

I know. Society certainly influenced who I portrayed
myself to be as a young girl. Girls today face different
pressures. But social influences still prompt girls to reach
for their masks—masks of indifference, people-pleasing
masks, or sometimes cold, spiteful masks—when what
they really want and need is warmth.

Like most girls, I wanted to do well in school. I wanted
to please the nuns who were my teachers, but I struggled.
It was not until years later, in college, when a professor
discovered I was dyslexic. So, in grade school, whether
spelling or math or science was the chore, my compre-
hension was poor. At home, though I'd like to have tried,
studying wasn't a priority. I had my brother to care for, and
the crash-bang-shout backdrop to contend with.

School was in one sense an oasis of normalcy. But along
with the approach of adolescence came the sting of bully's
taunts. While some girls began to grow curvy, my own

development lagged in that department. Dark, bushy underarm hair I grew in abundance; breasts, not so much.

I became the joke of the locker room—the hairy, flat-chested girl with big glasses and low grades.

My response was to add another layer to my mask, a protective layer, one that blocked others out.

Beneath that thickening mask was a girl very much in need of reassurance, a girl who possessed untapped talents, a girl who would grow into a strong, independent, well-educated, successful woman, wife and mother. It just took far longer to get there than it should have, over a path more perilous than it needed to be.

When I was developing *Changing the Chatter*, my daughter, Jennifer, was a huge inspiration and help to me throughout the process. She had supervised college retreats where she noticed female co-eds who clearly were hiding behind their masks. She said to me, "Mom, if they could learn how to take those masks off before college, their lives would be so much easier as freshmen."

Masks are a coping mechanism. They're also a lousy substitute for digging in and pulling problems out by the roots. The sooner girls learn to talk about their challenges, and not to mask either their pain or their potential, the better.

Changing the Chatter has a proven method for helping young girls to do just that, and to keep on doing it throughout their lives. Through small-group activities, exercises, and take-home audio-materials, ChatterGirls are equipped with the tools they need to show the world the truly wonderful, valuable, gifted people they really are.

Had I only enjoyed such an opportunity at their age, I could have shaved decades from my rise to self-awareness and fulfillment. But I can—and do—now take immense pleasure in helping young girls to gather the tools they need for what lies ahead.

"ChatterGirls helps you to look beyond what you feel like other people see," said Maddie. "And the activities are fun."

~ What matters is not what others think,
but what I know. ~

Chapter 11

Mind over Chatter

We all, at least occasionally, battle those inner voices that tell us we can't, we won't, we mustn't try, we're not smart enough, we're not pretty enough, it's out of reach, we just don't have what it takes.

For young girls, this internal racket can overwhelm. The messages girls receive from all angles can sting like arrows. Billboards, movies, magazines, the images on their phones and tablets, their peers—all are pitching them an endless stream of chatter, much of it creating a gnawing sense of inferiority.

I've been there. It's why I wore such a heavy mask for so very long. Without consistently encouraging parental influences in my young life, I allowed the harsh taunts of my peers to push me inward. I believed that what I saw in the mirror was gawky, that I'd never attract a boyfriend. The list went on.

The key is to change that chatter. We can work with young girls to help them to study the messages coming at them. Through *Changing the Chatter*, they learn not only to dismiss the negative, but also to re-craft what loops through their thoughts into positive chatter.

Our minds are like boxes, receptacles for all of our positive and negative chatter and thoughts. Trouble arises when we allow self-defeating messages to remain in the box, looping endlessly. Without the right tool for removing this negative chatter, we begin to believe it. That's corrosive. If permitted to continue, it rots the floor out from under our wellbeing.

With *Changing the Chatter*, we change what's in the box.
The girls learn to let go of the chatter that makes them feel
bad about themselves, to purge it and replace it with positive energy and chatter.

How do we do this? Each participating girl receives a
decorative box on the night when *Changing the Chatter* is
the topic. The girls write down words that sting, things
people have said that are hurtful, messages that have made
them feel sad or bad. They put the scraps of paper into
the box, and then they take those boxes and dump their
contents into a flowerpot.

We realize if we recycle paper and return it to the soil, we
will see growth take hold. The messages are the soil. The
girls are the seeds. The girls take these home as a reminder
that it is within their power to change ugly mind chatter
into beautiful thoughts and budding deeds. During the
last session, each girl receives her flower.

Sometimes, when an action is physical as well as mindful, its effects are more powerful and lasting.

In my own young life, I dealt with classmates who would say "Alicia, you're stupid. Don't you study?" That word—stupid—planted itself in my mind and it was very hard for me to let it go.

This activity of putting a word like "stupid" in a box and throwing it away says "I am not accepting of that; that is not who I am."

The girls also take their boxes home, hide them, and use them as needed to dispense with the negative, making room to build a library of positive thoughts in its place.

These girls learn how to make positive change now, and how to keep up with this great, freeing and invigorating habit for a lifetime.

"*Changing the Chatter* is a lesson Sofi still refers to now," said Emma, mother of 10-year-old Sofi, a ChatterGirl graduate of more than a year.

Emma enrolled Sofi in *Changing the Chatter* because Sofi had heard about it and was interested, and also because Sofi had been the victim of bullying at her grade school.

"Anywhere you go and no matter how old you are you hear negative chatter," Emma said. "It's an important lesson for anyone at any age."

For Sofi, the program was a Godsend, her mother said.

"It gives her the strength, when she does have rough days, to hold her head up higher," Emma said. "She now has the tools to deal with all of the negative stuff that's being thrown her way. There's no reason not to [enroll your daughter]."

Each of us faces difficult times. We encounter obstacles in our respective paths. But how we choose to shape the messages drifting (or hurtling) in our direction is truly up to us. If we establish strong self-esteem foundations in our daughters from an early age, they will be equipped to let go of the negative, to dwell instead on the positive, and to help others to do the same.

~ I am the girl with the strong, positive voice. ~

Chapter 12

Be Heard

Helping our daughters to find their voices starts with listening—truly listening—to what they have to say.

When your daughter speaks with you, are you fully engaged? Have you muted the TV set, put down the smart phone or tablet, and shut down for the moment your own distracting mental chatter?

Are you hearing what your daughter is saying, or are you checking off the tasks on your mental to-do list—wondering how long it will take to complete those chores yet to be done? Are you hearing her as your daughter tells you, for example, that two of her friends have decided to be boyfriend and girlfriend?

This could be an opening into a conversation about values, boundaries and self-respect. Simply by asking your daughter what she thinks that relationship status means, you may open the door to an eye-opening and fruitful dialogue. Daughters who know their parents' conversational door is open are less likely to absorb potentially harmful misinformation from "the street."

Truly listening teaches our daughters to do the same, and to be reflective. It also teaches them that their opinions and the points they make matter. We might not always be persuaded that what they are stating is in their own best interest, and as parents, of course, we make the house rules. But if we really want our daughters to grow, to develop strong voices, we also pay them the respect of telling them why we disagree when we do.

Changing the Chatter begins helping girls to find their voices from the very first session. Each session employs activity time not only to reinforce key points, but also to promote open dialogue between the participating girls.

During the My Voice session, the girls make seven colored bracelets, each bearing a letter from the words that comprise CHATTER: Celebrating, Happy, Aspiring, Truthful, Thoughtful, Esteem and Responsible. We talk about how developing each one of these traits strengthens their voices. Others recognize the strength of our voices through our actions.

We talk, for example, about the ways each of us celebrates life. Did we wake up this morning, smile and say to ourselves, "It's going to be a great day?"

Each of the bracelets is a different color, and the girls learn to associate the colors with the different traits and words, helping to cement the lessons in their minds. Blue is for

Celebrating, green for Happy, pink for Aspiring, yellow for Truthful, red for Thoughtful, purple for Esteem and orange for Responsible.

The girls also talk about times when they have felt they were not being heard, when others shut them down or when they simply feared that speaking up would be more trouble than it was worth.

This can be particularly key as youngsters approach middle school, a time when bullying tends to ramp up, and when anxiety might prevent one young girl from standing up for another.

At age 8, Sofi already had endured some bullying when she became involved in *Changing the Chatter: Celebrating ChatterGirls*.

"ChatterGirls has helped me to not be afraid to speak the truth when the truth is needed," said Sofi, 10 at the time of her interview for this book. "Now I can help other girls my age by talking with them about it."

The program presents a non-threatening environment in which participants can use their voices to discuss the various challenges of their young lives. If one has a relentlessly teasing older sibling who does not understand how much the teasing has affected her, and another faces a school bully, the rest of the group might ask questions and suggest ways to respond.

The conversation is valuable both to the ones releasing negativity and to those offering positive feedback. Feeling that others care is validating. Knowing that one's own caring nature can make a tremendous difference in the lives of others is an awakening.

ChatterGirls learn and practice these traits from the beginning to the end of each session. Each strengthens her individual voice while becoming part of a collective voice for strong, confident girls—and, eventually, for a successful, supportive network of women.

The importance of helping our daughters of today to keep—or find—their voices cannot be stressed strongly enough. Researchers Lyn Mikel Brown and Carol Gilligan, in a book called "Meeting at the Crossroads, Women's Psychology and Girls' Development," found that the path to womanhood is fraught with societal cues to become increasingly cautious, quiet and compliant.

Noted child and adolescent psychologist Martha Mendez-Baldwin also has gone on the record stating that young girls tend to go from gutsy to timid and yielding somewhere between grammar school and their early teens. As assertiveness wanes, confidence also too often tumbles.

It doesn't have to be that way.

In a "Fast Company" article by Gwen Moran—who sourced Mendez-Baldwin and the work of Mikel Brown and Gilligan as well as other experts in the field—five strong suggestions emerged. These are aimed at helping the adults in young girls' lives to thwart the loss-of-voice phenomenon.

Among them are encouraging her interests; pointing out media pressure, including social media; being mindful of the message your talk/criticism regarding your own appearance can send; allowing them a safe place to express themselves; and simply discussing with them the fact that this is something that can happen at their age.

All of these are bases covered throughout *Changing the Chatter.*

The results are both lasting and impressive.

"I still have the bracelets I made in ChatterGirls, and the little mirror. That sits on my dresser," said 13-year-old Maddie. "It reminds me to see myself as who I am on the inside. I also still have the box. It's hidden away in my closet.

"That's where the bad thoughts about myself go, like 'Oh, I'm never going to get very far with this,'" she continued. "I'm still a little shy, but I'll speak my mind when I feel that I should. If something's going on that I don't think is right, I will step in and say something."

Her sister, Anabelle, agreed that her ChatterGirls experience remains an important part of her life, and her voice.

"You might not think you need it," she said. "But in reality, I use what we learned there every day. I think it would help all girls to boost their confidence."

And 10-year-old Sofi, also among the first to complete the program in 2013, is sure that what she learned will help her to maintain her voice and strong sense of self-worth as she grows toward her dream of becoming an inventor, or perhaps a paleontologist.

"I would recommend it to other girls," Sofi said. "I can deal with problems better ... it's made me mentally stronger."

~ I become stronger when I claim my inner power. ~

Chapter 13

Land Outstanding Outcomes

Sofi's mother said enrolling her daughter in the *Changing the Chatter* program was among the best parenting decisions she has made.

"Sofi doesn't fit the scripted gender norms," she said. "She's not a girly girl. She doesn't wear nail polish. She doesn't swoon over One Direction. She's a hockey player and she's into science.

"She likes a lot of different things, but at the school she was going to, girls were supposed to be cookie-cutter—love One Direction, paint their nails, talk about fashion. She would get harassed for not fitting that mold.

"A lot of the things she was learning at ChatterGirls—about being comfortable with who she was, being proud of liking different things and not being a two-dimensional cookie-cutter person—she was able to put into action right away," the mom said. "It helped her to hear an adult she admired say 'No, Sofi, you're good. Keep being you.' It really helped her a lot and gave her that extra boost of confidence."

Emma, Sofi's mother, said that she was thrilled with the way *Changing the Chatter* helped Sofi to become much more shielded against the negative effects of bullying. Emma often volunteers with youth-oriented groups and witnesses first-hand the devastating effects bullying can have on any child, she said.

"The program gave Sofi the tools to stand strong against negativity," Emma said. "It also gave her the tools to not become a negative person herself. Bullying is a constant thing. There's no way to ignore it. But this ensures that my daughter is not going to become a bully.

"If she feels this confident about herself and understands her own value, that makes her a more compassionate person," Emma continued.

Emma said she wishes all young girls could enjoy the benefits of *Changing the Chatter*.

"It's harder to retrain once you're older and you've gotten more set in your ways—if you've been hurt and damaged and have the scars," she said. "If we can almost inoculate these children and give them these good habits while they're younger, they'll be more resilient.

"Hopefully Sofi will be able to get through these tough years coming up in middle school and high school a little bit more smoothly," Emma said. "It's sort of like being pre-armed."

Kelly, the mother of Anabelle and Maddie, beamed as she listened to her daughters describe how ChatterGirls continued to play a key role in their lives years after their sessions.

"A lot of girls judge themselves on how they look," Kelly's 11-year-old said. "They think they're not good enough if they don't look pretty. ChatterGirls helps them to see that looks don't really matter, and to look inside to see who they are.

"I'm someone who is funny and nice and not mean."

"ChatterGirls gives you the confidence to say 'I can do this,'" added Kelly's older daughter, Maddie. "It helps you to stand up for yourself. There are some girls out there who I know are struggling. They bully because their home life is bad. You can feel better about it all when you learn about it."

The younger girl, Anabelle, said the program has helped her not only to deflect unwarranted criticism, but also to stand up for others.

"Before, I might have said, 'It's none of my business. It's not my problem,'" she said. "Now if I notice people struggling, I try to help them out."

~ I realize my uniqueness.
I develop it. I celebrate it.
I use it to fuel my self-esteem
and to change the world. ~

Chapter 14

Make A Difference

Riley was 9 years old when she became a ChatterGirl. A year later, she recalled feeling a bit anxious before the first session.

"I was not feeling like I fit in," she said. "I felt like nobody was going to like me. But the room was filled with girls just like me. I learned I don't have to be in the shadows."

Riley said she still has her mirror and her mask and she continues to journal —another key component of *Changing the Chatter*. Like other program graduates, she also makes frequent use of her CDs.

"I listen to them 217 days out of 365," the precocious 10-year-old said. "I feel like I'm a better person from ChatterGirls."

In fact, as I write this book, Riley is looking forward to her 11th birthday, so she can take the program again as part of the older girls' group.

Riley's mother, Sarah, said her daughter came away from each session happy and excited to talk about what she did at *Changing the Chatter*, and what she got to bring home. With each passing week, Riley's self-reliance and confidence grew.

The program works, helping young girls to feel great about themselves so that they are more secure about revealing their true natures to the world, the mom said. Participants learn to encourage one another from the start in a safe, comfortable and nonjudgmental setting.

"Not only is it financially doable, but the girls are spending a lot of time doing and learning, not sitting there being talked at," Sarah said. "It's definitely been a positive experience. She wants to go back."

Riley said she used to feel a bit like a misfit; she didn't fit the cheerleader mold nor was she part of an "in" crowd at school. Now she chats happily about her sewing skills, her mind for math and science, and how much she enjoys swim team practice, Irish dancing, art and music.

In short, she's pretty great, and she's no longer in the shadows, afraid to show it. *Changing the Chatter* was key for Riley, and can be for all young girls.

"It's like having magic powers that you use only for good," said Riley, who aspires to be a doctor or surgeon one day. "It teaches younger girls to have enthusiasm and courage, to speak up to bullies and to put up your game … it makes me feel comfortable around other people."

Helping young girls to achieve that comfort level—within themselves and around others—has been so tremendously gratifying. We've made a great, impactful start, but there's so much more we can do.

That is why I am devoted to expanding the program's sphere, enabling caring leaders across the country to experience these same highly desirable and fantastic outcomes. The women of tomorrow deserve it. They deserve to arrive at adulthood's door with a strong, clear sense of self, and the confidence to share their gifts with the world.

"There's not a single person who cannot benefit from this kind of program," said Emma, mother of ChatterGirl Sofi. "Every woman has people out there trying to stab her in the back. Look at women on TV. If they're not being objectified, they're being called bossy or bitchy because they're trying to take control.

"ChatterGirls was so well worth it for Sofi," Emma continued. "It's something that has stuck with her."

~ I have the power within to accomplish great things. ~

Chapter 15

Walk the Talk

Throughout the program, students often ask, "Miss Alicia, why are you doing this? Why did you start this program? Why is it so important to you?"

Our focus during all sessions is on the girls. And having the high school-aged leaders in the room is so beneficial. They've just emerged from middle school and often relate with precisely what their younger counterparts are experiencing, offering useful tips on how they overcame challenges.

I relate, too, as the girls eventually come to learn—but not until the final night, during the 100 Percent ME session.

We talk during 100 Percent ME about the girls and the pictures that they drew during Mirror Mirror, on the first night. I pull out a picture of me when I was 7 or 8, with a big-toothed grin and flipped short hair, and I ask the girls, "What do you think is going on in that girl's mind?"

Do they think I liked the way I looked? Was I happy? Did I defend myself against bullies? Did I like who I was on the inside?

No, no, no and no.

Perhaps when the girls in the room started their ChatterGirls journey, they had some of those same negative feelings toward themselves.

But there's a key difference between them and me: They're now equipped with the tools they need to change their negative chatter, to replace it with positive self-talk before it festers.

The lack of acquiring this skill set at their age was, for me and for so many women, profoundly difficult to overcome. I know now that it delayed my path to success by decades. That's why I developed *Changing the Chatter*, why it's so vitally important to me. No girl should by stymied in this altogether preventable way. All are worthy of learning how to change the chatter while it matters, to build their confidence, express their strengths.

The girls and I talk about waking up each morning, looking in the mirror and seeing ourselves for the incredibly talented, beautiful and valuable people that we are—inside and out.

I encourage the girls to ask themselves each morning, "Will I choose to hide behind my mask today? Or will I choose to take it off and use my voice? What change will I make today? What noise do I have to stop to have my voice?"

The girls write letters to themselves about how much they like themselves and what they like about themselves.

Toward the end of the evening, there's some fun time. We have nail polish for the girls who enjoy that, and colored hair extensions and hair clips.

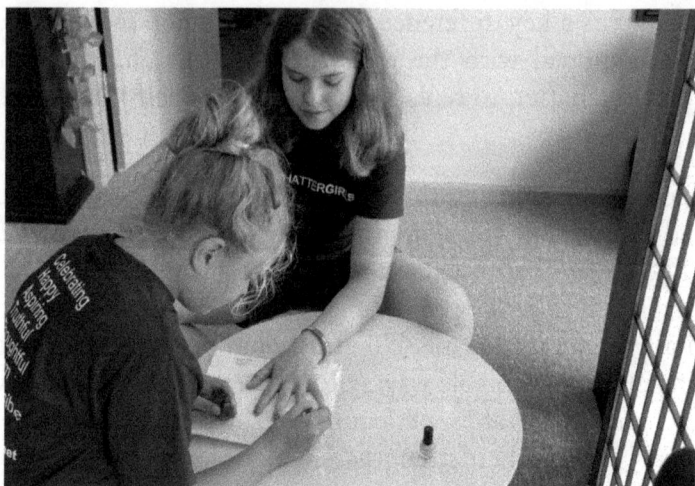

We talk about the image they saw in the mirror during the first session as they prepare for a final-night photo and short video. How does that image differ from the person here tonight?

Time is reserved for each girl to emerge from behind a curtain and to be filmed introducing herself and talking about who she is for a few minutes. Each ends her talk with "I'm a ChatterGirl."

It's graduation night, and the message is clear: Each ChatterGirl is beautiful and will become a strong, confident woman. She needs only to open her new toolbox whenever it's called for.

When the girls leave that night, they take with them an empty picture frame, but no CD. Thirty days later, they receive their final CD, along with their photo, their letter to themselves and a letter from me.

In the future, I hope thousands of ChatterGirls leaders are sending such letters.

Moms tell me the girls are so eager to receive this parcel that they visit the mailbox daily, peppering their parents with "When is it coming?"

How wonderful it is to know that the girls anticipate and appreciate this lasting reminder of their time in *Changing the Chatter: Celebrating ChatterGirls*. How wonderful to envision this opportunity being afforded to girls everywhere—so that the true gift of *Changing the Chatter* will be witnessed across the workplaces, boardrooms and families of the future.

~ Others hurt me only when I give them the power. ~

Chapter 16

Apply the Science

Study after study has shown that low self-esteem is linked with substance and/or alcohol abuse, reduced success at school and work, relationship failures, depression and worse.

A variety of clinical psychologists with pediatric specialties have determined that, when it comes to our girls, those with high self-esteem are far more likely to delay sexual intercourse, complete school, avoid eating disorders, and generally live happier, healthier, more productive lives.

So, we've talked a lot about self-esteem. But what is it, exactly? And why should parents, educators—all of us, really—place great emphasis on its importance during child development and pre-adolescence?

British author, life coach and personal development trainer Paul Ogunkoya established and administers a website called self-esteem-school.com. He offers this definition of self-esteem: "The perception you hold about yourself as an individual, the beliefs you have about yourself with regard to what you can achieve and your ability to deal with the daily pressures of life."

Changing the Chatter recognizes that self-esteem issues vary widely depending on gender. It aims to equip young girls from 8 to 14 with the tools they need to perceive themselves as highly valuable individuals, to always believe in their capacity to achieve, and to establish a healthy pattern for dealing with life's daily pressures.

The World Health Organization, the U.S. Centers for Disease Control and other highly regarded experts agree that women are far more likely to suffer from anxiety and depression than men. Physician and author Ruta Nonacs says about one in four women suffer from depression at some point.

In her book "A Deeper Shade of Blue: A Woman's Guide to Recognizing and Treating Depression in Her Child-bearing Years," Nonacs notes that prior to adolescence, rates of depression are nearly equal between girls and boys.

"Things begin to shift between the ages of 11 and 13," she wrote. "Over these years, there is a dramatic rise in the prevalence of depression in girls, and by the age of 15, females are twice as likely as males to suffer from depresion.

"What happens to create this gender gap during adolescence is a topic of intense debate and research," her book continues. "There is no doubt that adolescence is a time characterized by dramatic psychological and physical changes for women, and it is easy to imagine that this tumultuous transition may render adolescent girls more vulnerable to depression.

"However, a woman's risk for depression persists beyond puberty ..."

Females' greater hormonal fluctuations—in combination with the stress of balancing education, career and child-rearing—likely play a role in the statistical disparity, experts suggest.

We certainly can't and don't promise that all Chatter-Girl graduates will journey through life utterly free of depression or anxiety. But we know that building that all-important self-esteem foundation during the critical 8- to 14-year-old time period will mentally equip our daughters to face with moxie the challenges ahead.

ChatterGirls learn how to press the stop-and-clear button when negative chatter threatens to replay within their minds. They are mindful that their worth is measured by so much more than their outward appearance. They set aside the masks that otherwise might hide their true—and truly wonderful—identities. They achieve the ability to sit quietly and meditatively.

They also discover the value of journaling, the bounty of boosting others when they are down, and the treasure of speaking in full, confident voice. Most importantly, they gain not only self-acceptance; the goal is self-love.

The magnitude of this breakthrough cannot be overstated. The mother of 10-year-old Sofi put it perfectly.

"Sofi has the sense now of thinking 'If I have this inherent value, then you must have this inherent value as well,'" Emma said.

Indeed, there is little regard for others without regard for self.

*~ Today, I can spark a current of
positivity that goes on and on. ~*

Chapter 17

Build Alliances

Any parent reading this book obviously is a caring one. Some might be struggling with their daughters, while others simply wish to do all they can to enhance their child's chances for success.

Parents don't remain on the premises during ChatterGirls sessions, thus freeing the participants to be more open about the challenges they face than they might otherwise be.

However, were a parent a fly on the wall, she'd spy smiling girls enjoying one another's company and paving their way toward powerful self-reliance and potent empathy.

"I'm happy," said a smiling 8-year-old girl at the start of one session. Long, blonde locks swaying, she jumped up and down a few times before kneeling on one of several large, fluffy pillows spread out on the carpet.

"Did everyone take home their CD last week?" the leader asked.

"Yes!" a group of six girls replied.

"How was your week, Miss Sarah?" the instructor continued.

Just a few short weeks in to the ChatterGirls experience, a group of strangers has become a group of friends and allies. These girls have shared not only confidences, but also emotional minefield strategies. Together, they're conquering weaknesses and building strengths.

In Chapter 11, we delved into why this self-esteem-building practice is so key for our daughters. Sometimes I'm asked, "Don't boys face challenges, too?" Of course. But there can be no doubt that the game is rigged differently when it comes to the fallout of a missed foundational opportunity.

Like it or not, the societal emphasis on appearance equaling value is so much more pervasive for girls. Whereas the nerdy, bookish boy may grow up to found the Googles and Facebooks of the world, the girl with the high IQ and low fashion sense will suffer the confidence-busting effects of being an outcast right into adulthood.

We may say to ourselves, "Oh, this is no longer true, not in modern society." I wish that were so.

Yes, we've made strides. More than ever, today's female celebrities consist of all shapes and sizes. But let's face it. Society still inflicts its unrealistic standards of the ideal body shape, its definition of "beauty." And girls, far more than boys, are victimized when they don't fit the mold.

If we as parents and guardians don't take the time, at the right time, to work with our daughters to instill in them the sense of their inherent value as human beings, perils loom. Anorexia. Bulimia. Substance abuse. Cutting. Promiscuity. The list goes on.

Middle school is a minefield. Classmates can be downright mean.

A young girl may think to herself, "I don't fit into any of these molds. I don't know where I'm going and I don't know what to do about it."

One of the greatest things about *Changing the Chatter* is its complement of high-school-aged volunteers who are there to let the younger girls know that it gets better. Young girls who encounter these challenges without anyone to help them learn to counter them can continue to carry difficulties into high school and beyond.

We've all heard the stories about girls as young as 16 having breast augmentation and other plastic surgeries. These girls have parents who are so desperate to help them to feel better about themselves that they support their physical alterations. In reality, the change that's needed lies within.

True inner happiness isn't about appearance or the judgment of others. It's about inner strength and acceptance of self.

Sure, we always want to improve ourselves. We might want a new hairdo or desire a flattering outfit. We might wish to become more physically fit and make better nutritional choices. There's nothing wrong with any of that, if we're doing it for ourselves first and not simply to please others.

Helping our daughters to learn while they're young how to change negative mental chatter into positive, self-affirming thoughts is so key. Among other poor choices, women who lack inner strength, esteem and confidence so often choose men who have expectations having little or nothing to do with who they are.

While the perfect relationship may not exist, the only way we'll ever come close is first to really get to know and accept ourselves.

Often, the first sign of trouble with a young girl is falling grades or withdrawal. A teacher may notice struggle and call a parent. Among the first questions may be "What's happening at home? Is there a divorce pending?"

Sometimes it has nothing to do with a child's home life. Something is happening in that girl's mind concerning where she believes she belongs. As part of the *Changing the Chatter* program, lines of communication are open with parents. We meet before the program starts, and we talk about the sorts of things girls between 8 and 14 are beginning to hear within their minds.

Once a girl is 13 or 14, she often has entered the "I don't want to talk about it" arena. A parent can wind up on the sidelines going "What happened to my daughter?"

Parental support is key throughout *Changing the Chatter: Celebrating ChatterGirls*. Participants come away with the best possible outcomes when mom or dad is encouraging them, asking them about the CDs or setting aside time for them to journal even after they leave the program.

Encouraging the girls to continue to use their *Changing the Chatter* tools is important. Throughout the program, parents receive weekly emails briefly detailing the theme and key points of each session—plus suggested questions to ask their daughters to advance the conversation.

Parents are reminded that a peaceful action like drawing a picture or shutting the bedroom door to listen to a CD can allow a child to make a change that she can own.

It's about empowerment. Lifelong empowerment.

~ The chatter I allow in my mind is the positive chatter. ~

Chapter 18

Visualize the Rise

A key takeaway from the *Changing the Chatter* method is the ability to quiet one's mind—to shut off the noise of the world, travel to a place of peace and hone in on inner thoughts.

Very few programs lead girls on anything similar to what we call "Journey to the Mind". This visualization technique helps them to learn to listen to themselves, pair positive thoughts with their identities, and dispense with the negative.

As we "Journey to the Mind" during the important *Changing the Chatter* session, each girl learns to draw an inward picture of what a negative thought looks like to them, and how a positive thought appears. Sometimes, these ideas become things; other times they are just colors.

One girl might paint her positive thoughts all in white and her negatives in gray. For others, it's beautiful pastels against darkness.

Each one takes ownership of her positive and negative chatter, and learns how to embrace the positive while putting the negative in a box where it loses all power, and eventually is disposed of.

In learning to paint their own mental pictures of their chatter, they adopt individual means of taking charge of their thoughts. What others say and do is beyond our control. But how we manifest what others say and do is very much within our control. We can choose to accept only that which is supportive and encouraging and beneficial, and we can be supportive, encouraging, positive friends to others.

When we quiet the chatter inside our minds and work to strengthen the positive message, we're stronger.

Every day, each of us will go up against something scary, some unknown, some situation that makes us anxious. But ChatterGirls have adopted certain tenets: Belief in self, strength in voice, and a unique ability to thwart the negative. A ChatterGirl knows she's valuable, and acknowledges the value in others.

She makes new and valuable friendships, often meeting girls from other schools or towns. Session participants may walk in to the first meeting as strangers, but within the first hour, they're laughing and connecting. Their struggles are similar. They have a common base from which to form a bond.

Some of the girls who attend have been bullied to the point of growing withdrawn. Some might feel as though their only friends are their parents. And some have reached a point where they aren't very forthcoming about their challenges. Their parents sense they're struggling, but aren't quite sure why, and they may feel powerless to help.

Changing the Chatter not only equips those attending with the tools they need to meet and overcome the trials of adolescence, it also equips parents with questions and tools for following up. In this way, and through continued use of the CDs and practice of the lessons, the program does not end after the fifth session. Its effects are ongoing.

Changing the Chatter can help tomorrow's women to be unabashedly ready to contribute to the world's wonders. And so can you.

Excited yet?

~ Every day I remind myself of my own inherent quality.
I know that I was created to give of my talents
to make the world a better place. ~

Chapter 19

Nix Negativity

It's so interesting to look at the past. As young parents, many of us start out thinking "I'm not going to do or say any of the hurtful things my parents did and said while I was growing up. I will do better. I do not want to repeat the mistakes that trouble me to this day."

As hard as we may try, though, we often repeat at least part of a negative cycle. The way we are raised greatly affects our parental instincts. Avoiding that which can emotionally harm isn't always easy, though we have the best of intentions. It can take generations of effort.

Being a parent, whether married or single, is an awesome responsibility. We carry the potential to assist a child in growing and maturing in a positive way.

For some, the skill set may be lacking. And it's OK to find groups or individuals who can help us to become better parents. It's OK, in fact it's important, to realize that your child's world is a different place than the one in which you grew up. The parenting "manual" for each of us looks different.

Any young girl's outlook as she tries to find her place in the world looks different from that of every other girl. Genetics. Chemistry. Nurturing. It all comes into play.

I love watching the girls grow and change throughout the ChatterGirls sessions. *Changing the Chatter* allows them to shut off the world and look inside and figure out who they really are. "Journey to the Mind" is a meditative state, something most of the girls—and more than a few of their parents—have not previously experienced.

The girls learn to stop external stimuli for a time, to look inward, and to focus on their mental chatter, recognizing the positive from the negative. When your child begins to talk with you about the chatter, we begin to see change.

Any parent can say to a child, "Stand up to the bully." But we may fail to recognize that the chatter sometimes renders a child powerless.

We send our children off to school believing they'll be OK. But when anxiety sets in and sadness creeps toward withdrawal, the poor grades arrive. Parents may feel unprepared to deal with what is happening. In *Changing the Chatter*, we realize that during this phase of development, young girls want to handle their difficulties themselves. And some can.

Others struggle. And what we find is that, even years later in high school or college, or even adulthood, they strive but cannot overcome feelings of powerlessness. They never learned what to do with the negativity swirling in their minds, its defeating effects unabated.

Some may eventually find their inner strength. Others will face a rockier journey.

Taking 10 minutes to shut off the world—shut off the phones, the TV, etc.—a child has the opportunity to go within and stop the chatter. Give the power to go within to a 9-year-old, and you have given her the chance at a far smoother path.

When I was a child, prayer time served as my only quiet, inwardly focused time. I grew to realize that these were the only moments when I really stopped the chatter, shut life off and searched for the positive.

As parents, we must set the example and teach our children to go within, examine their thoughts and take control of the ones that stand in their way.

As a coach and counselor, I see so many children struggling through the thoughts that morph into anxiety, headaches, sadness, and self-destructive behaviors that they feel powerless to stop.

We teach children simple math by repetitive drills. We too often, however, do not attempt to teach them how to stop the thoughts that defy their needs until serious problems arise.

Getting help when it is needed is, of course, the right thing to do. Better yet, though, is prevention. We all have the power inside to change and to accept or reject negative thoughts. Throughout *Changing the Chatter*, we affirm and reaffirm that power—before the bottom falls out.

Just as one might do multiplication table drills, we employ repetition to instill ChatterGirls life skills. "Journey to the Mind" reminds each participant that she has the tools to improve her mindset, and to maintain a healthy one. Reminding her that she has these tools is a lot easier than watching anxiety levels spiral out of control.

While we practice repetition in *Changing the Chatter*, it's important for parents to remind their daughters to keep using the mental tools they now have on hand.

Equipping our daughters with these all-important tools during the crucial 8- to 14-year-old time span can make all the difference in her experiences throughout high school and beyond. Rather than becoming helicopter parents, or falling back on less-than-stellar traits of our own upbringing, we can enable tomorrow's young women to think for themselves.

We can teach them to shut off the chatter that damages and to embrace the chatter that builds.

The pattern of repeating parents' mistakes can be so hard to break. For example, my mom and dad were yellers, and when I was a young mom, I found myself frequently yelling at my daughter. When I realized what I was doing, I worked very hard to change it.

As parents, we have to learn to allow children opportunities to do their own work as they develop—with guidance, not interference, yelling or worse. How else can they understand the concept of consequences?

Moms and dads of 8- to 14-year-olds, you've arrived at a time when you're witnessing your little girl develop into a young woman. If you want her to carry positive traits into adulthood and to discontinue any negative family cycles, help her to realize that she has the power within.

She can make changes now that will enable her to be a woman of strength from the onset. Or, she can make changes at 40, having spent decades floundering in the pitfalls of self-defeating habits and passing them on to a new generation.

It is my mission to see all young girls gain the opportunity to develop the positive mindset skill set that *Changing the Chatter* offers.

~ The positive energy I generate flows through me to others—and then from them to still more. ~

Chapter 20

Take a Stand

I believe that every young girl should have the opportunity to acquire the tools necessary to follow a confident, self-assured path into adulthood.

This movement is all about changing the chatter, altering the soup of thoughts swirling within young girls' minds so that only the nutritious bits remain. Much like a rotten recipe ingredient, thoughts that don't feed hearts and fuel growth aren't allowed in the mix.

Taking negative thoughts and turning them into positive, self-esteem-building reflections might sound like an overly simplistic solution to a complex problem. But, with the right skills, it is not only possible, it's also potentially life-changing. All our girls need are the proper tool sets, and great guidance on how to use them.

Changing the Chatter offers just that. We hope you will help spread awareness of this program—perhaps even start a division of it in your region—so that the girls of today may be better-equipped to grow into the confident leaders of tomorrow.

Whatever she chooses to pursue, from parenting or piloting to paleontology, a ChatterGirl recognizes her inherent worth, speaks firmly and knows that setbacks do not equal failures.

We can help girls learn how to muster their inner strengths today, tomorrow and throughout their lives. It is my hope, indeed my mission, to encourage other women to learn the ChatterGirls process and invest in teaching it to young girls throughout the world.

Just imagine what a tremendous difference you might make in the futures of young girls in your community.

To learn more, visit chattergirls.net.

~ A strong voice proclaims that I can have anything in the way of a career—or in life. I am the girl with the strong, positive voice. I will be the person in the world who shows compassion and understanding of others, because when I speak, my heart does, too. ~

About Alicia Marcos Birong

Alicia is the founder and owner of *Changing the Chatter: Celebrating ChatterGirls* and Guided Choices.

With a passion for improving and empowering the lives of individuals of all ages, she has worked with children and adults for over 30 years as a life coach, therapist and hypnotherapist. Alicia holds a master's degree in counseling from Loyola University in Chicago.

Throughout her career Alicia has worked in the nonprofit arena, the business community, and the Catholic Church. She also teaches pediatric hypnotherapy at conferences and to therapists in the Chicago area, has published various articles, and has presented the topic to both national and international audiences.

Alicia started *Changing the Chatter: Celebrating Chatter-Girls* in 2013 to help young girls between the ages of 8 and 14 deal with social pressures and self-esteem issues. The goal today is to spread the message across the nation so young girls will have the tools they need to be stronger, more confident young women. In acknowledgement of *Changing the Chatter: Celebrating ChatterGirls*, Shaw Media awarded Alicia with a Hometown Heroes Award, given to residents who have made a marked contribution to their community.

Alicia resides in the Chicago area with her husband, Bill. She is the mother of two successful, grown children, and also is a proud grandmother.

You can contact Alicia at aliciachattergirls@gmail.com or 815-404-8343.

Learn more about Alicia at www.guidedchoices.com.

For more information on *Changing the Chatter: Celebrating ChatterGirls*, visit www.chattergirls.net or find it on Facebook, Twitter or Instagram.

Changing the Chatter: Help Your Daughter Look Beyond the Mirror for Self-Esteem was written in collaboration with Cynthia Wolf of Wolf Wordsmithing.